Usborne
Dinosaur Mazes

Illustrated by
Valeria Danilova, Susanna Rumiz,
The Boy Fitz Hammond, Mattia Cerato
and Wesley Robins

Designed by Claire Thomas

Written by Sam Smith

The mazes at the beginning of the
book are easier and they get more
challenging as you go through.
You'll find solutions to all of
them on pages 61-64.

Hot-spring hatchlings

Can you help the Ferganasaurus mother make her way between these hot spring pools so she can look after her hatching babies?

Mother

Mud muddle

One young Sinornithomimus has slipped and become trapped in a pool of thick, sticky mud. Which path does his friend need to hurry along to help pull him free?

START

Seafood supper

Pick out the air current that the Pteranodon should soar along to return to the cliffside cave and deliver a fishy meal to the hungry fledgling.

START

Desk directions

Find Peter a clear path through the laboratory, between the fossils and his fellow scientists, so he can examine the new dinosaur skull that has just been delivered to his desk.

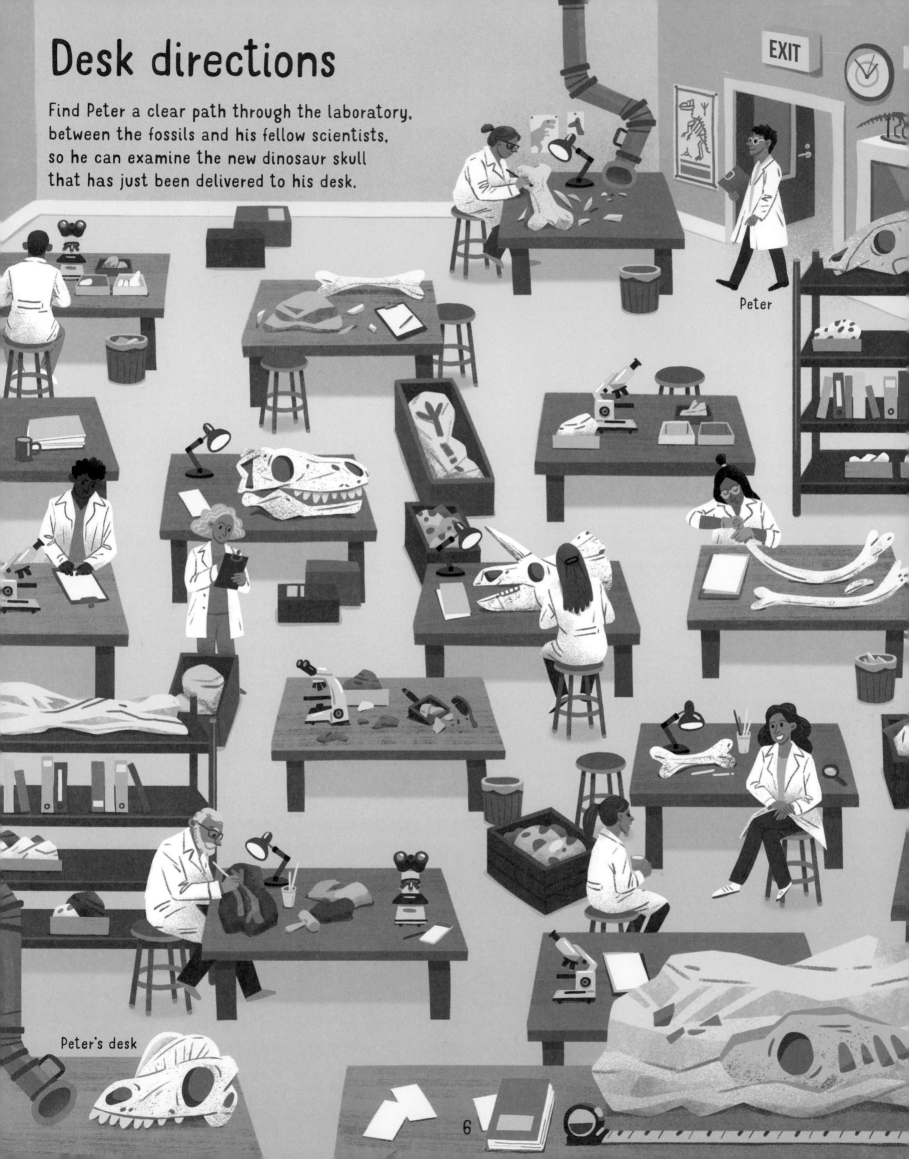

EXIT

Peter

Peter's desk

Forest fright

These panicked plant-eaters are fleeing from a T. rex trampling through the forest. Can you lead the Struthiomimus safely through to the front of the stampede?

START

FINISH

Quetzalcoatlus quest

Help the Quetzalcoatlus mother find a clear route back between the rocks and her friends to check on her eggs before they hatch. Hers are the only ones that have white spots.

Mother

Cave cover

Lead the yellow Ankylosaurus along the hilltop paths to the last empty cave to shelter from the storm and the flashing forks of lightning.

START

Woodland walk

Can you help this Caudipteryx find a way through the crowded forest, between the leaves, logs and other dinosaurs, to reach the quieter clearing?

START

Clearing

Crowded coast

Find the little fish a way up from the bottom of the sea to swim with its friend near the sunny surface. (It must stay underwater at all times.)

FINISH

START

Lake reunion

Lead the thirsty Hadrosaurus along a clear path through the ferns and flowering plants to rejoin the rest of the family and take a cool drink from the lake.

FINISH

START

13

Finding fossils

Pick out a path through this dig site so Percy can help his friends finish unearthing the huge dinosaur fossil. He wants to refill his bottle at the red water cooler along the way, but don't take him anywhere twice.

Percy

FINISH

15

Swim to the surface

The hungry Pliosaurus has dived down to look for lunch, but now it needs to breathe. Which way should it swim up to resurface, and take a big gulp of fresh air?

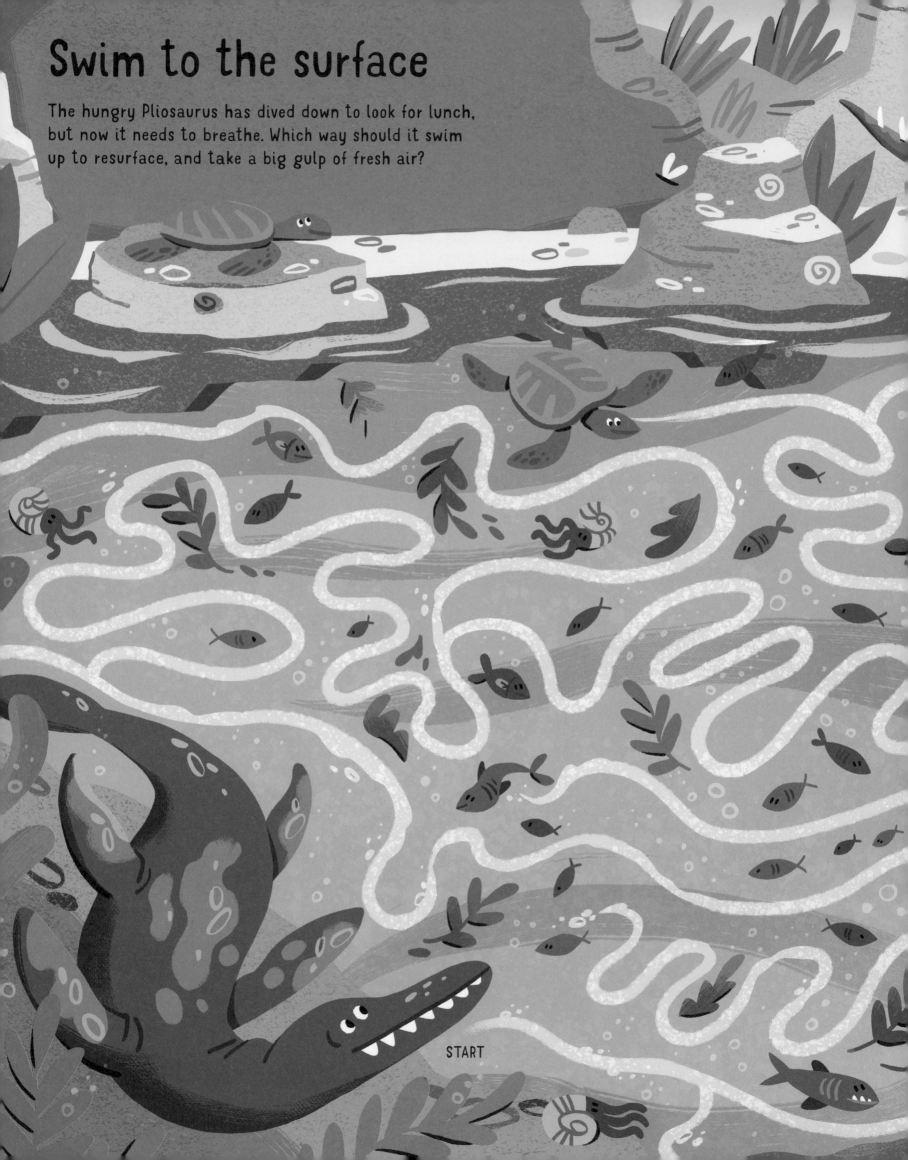

START

FINISH

17

Tree climber

Can you find the Epidexipteryx a way to climb to the top of this tree, without taking the risk of slipping on any of the slimy moss?

FINISH

START

Fossilized footprints

These scientists are close to discovering a new dinosaur specimen at their dig site. Help Fiona follow the right trail of fossilized footprints to find it. Then circle the species that the specimen belongs to on the guide.

Fiona

DIPLODOCUS STEGOSAURUS ALLOSAURUS

FOOTPRINTS GUIDE

19

Picky plant-eater

Guide the hungry Triceratops around the rocks and the rest of the herd to snack on the lush leaves of the tastiest, untouched plants.

FINISH

START

Tinodon trails

Help the Tinodon scurry along the right path between the forest ferns to reach the base of the tall tree's trunk.

FINISH

START

22

Going underground

Guide the orange Oryctodromeus underground, through the network of tunnels, to reach the nesting infants. Avoid the other adults as they won't be happy with another dinosaur barging into their burrows.

START

FINISH

Twilight trouble

Night is falling fast and it's not safe to be out in the open. Which paths should the Prenocephale sneak along to reach the cave without being seen by any of the vicious Velociraptors who are on the hunt?

START

River route

Can you find the family of fish a safe route along the unblocked streams and rivers? They need to reach the lake without being spotted by any of the beady-eyed Baryonyx.

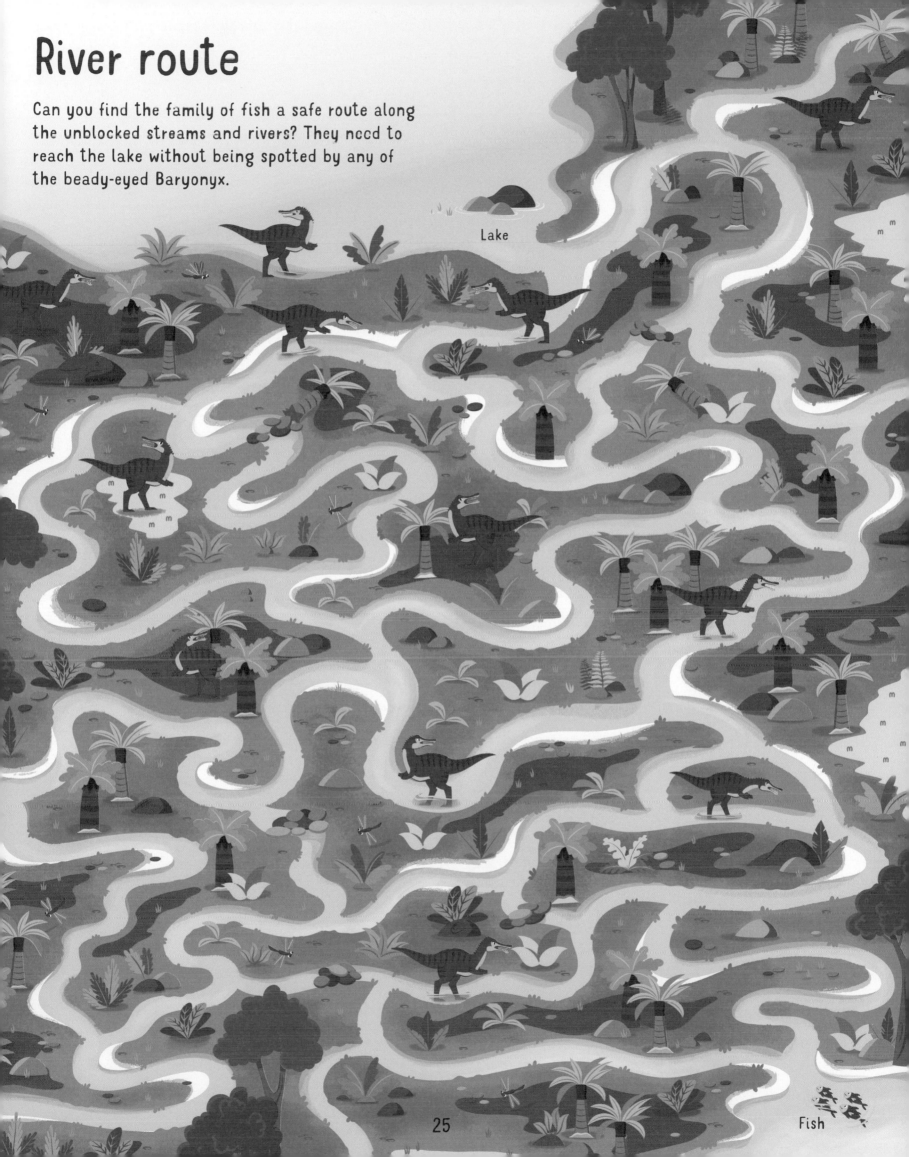

Lake

Fish

Smoky skies

Which way along the warm air currents should the pterosaur fly to find a way up to clearer skies? It's not safe to fly through the toxic clouds of fumes billowing from the volcanoes.

FINISH

START

Flash floods

Can you pick out a dry path for the purple dinosaur to cross these flooded lands and return to the rest of the herd?

START

The herd

27

Wintry waters

Lead the Leaellynasaura through the frozen forest to take a refreshing drink from the running water of the stream. Be sure to keep to the paths that others have cleared in the shallower snow.

START

FINISH

29

Weary wanderers

Which way should the weary herd of Stegosaurus plod across the plain, around the rocks, plants and other dinosaurs, so they can cool off at the watering hole?

The herd

FINISH

Cave course

Which way does the nautilus need to travel through these underwater caves to rise to the surface for a night-time feed?

FINISH

START

Missing Maiasaura

Two members of the Maiasaura herd have fallen behind. Can you find them a route through the rocky canyon to catch up, keeping clear of any predators who are on the lookout for lunch?

This is a predator.

The herd

START

Dinosaur museum

Can you lead Lizzie and Larry through this dinosaur museum to peruse the prehistoric attractions? They want to visit all of the rooms just once, without retracing their steps.

ENTRANCE

Lizzie and Larry

EXIT

35

Canyon crisis

Can you guide the Parasaurolophus quickly through the canyon to protect the eggs from the hungry Pteranodons who are circling overhead?

START

37

Sauropod search

The purple sauropod is looking for her son, who has wandered off in search of a snack. He's still too short to see from far away, so lead her along a clear path through the forest to find him.

START

Son

Earthquake escape

An earthquake has opened up these huge gaps in the ground. Can you help the red Lystrosaurus find a way back between the cracks and crevices to safety?

START

FINISH

Wade through the water

Can you guide the baby Charonosaurus back along the shallow paths through the watering hole so he can share a refreshing drink with his dad?

Baby

Dad

Glade glider

Which way must the Changyuraptor glide down, through the forest foliage, to reach the eggs and help them hatch?

START

Meteorite strike

Small meteorites have started raining down around these dinosaurs. Can you help the Noasaurus hurry along the right route to reach the cave and take cover?

START

Mangrove meal

Which way should the Spinosaurus swim through these salty waters to snap up all the fish and return to where it started, without going anywhere twice?

START

Forest feeders

The Edmontosaurus herd's forest feeding ground has been set on fire by a nearby volcano. Lead them across the landscape to find a new forest, taking care to avoid any Tyrannosaurus lying in wait along the way.

This is a Tyrannosaurus.

FINISH

The herd

Crater confusion

The young yellow dinosaur wandered down into this deep crater but is now lost. Can you help it find the way back up to the top?

START

FINISH

Prehistoric Park

Show Anna and Amy around Prehistoric Park so they can see all the dinosaur exhibits and read every red information sign before making their way back to where they began, without doubling back.

Anna and Amy

WELCOME

Lagoon lunch

Can you find the Compsognathus a route through the lagoon, snapping up all six little blue lizards on the way, without taking any path twice?

START

FINISH

51

Dangerous descent

This volcano is pouring out streams of liquid lava, leaving these dinosaurs in precarious positions. Can you help the Plateosaurus pick out a path down the mountainside, avoiding the molten rock, to find a way to the foothills?

FINISH

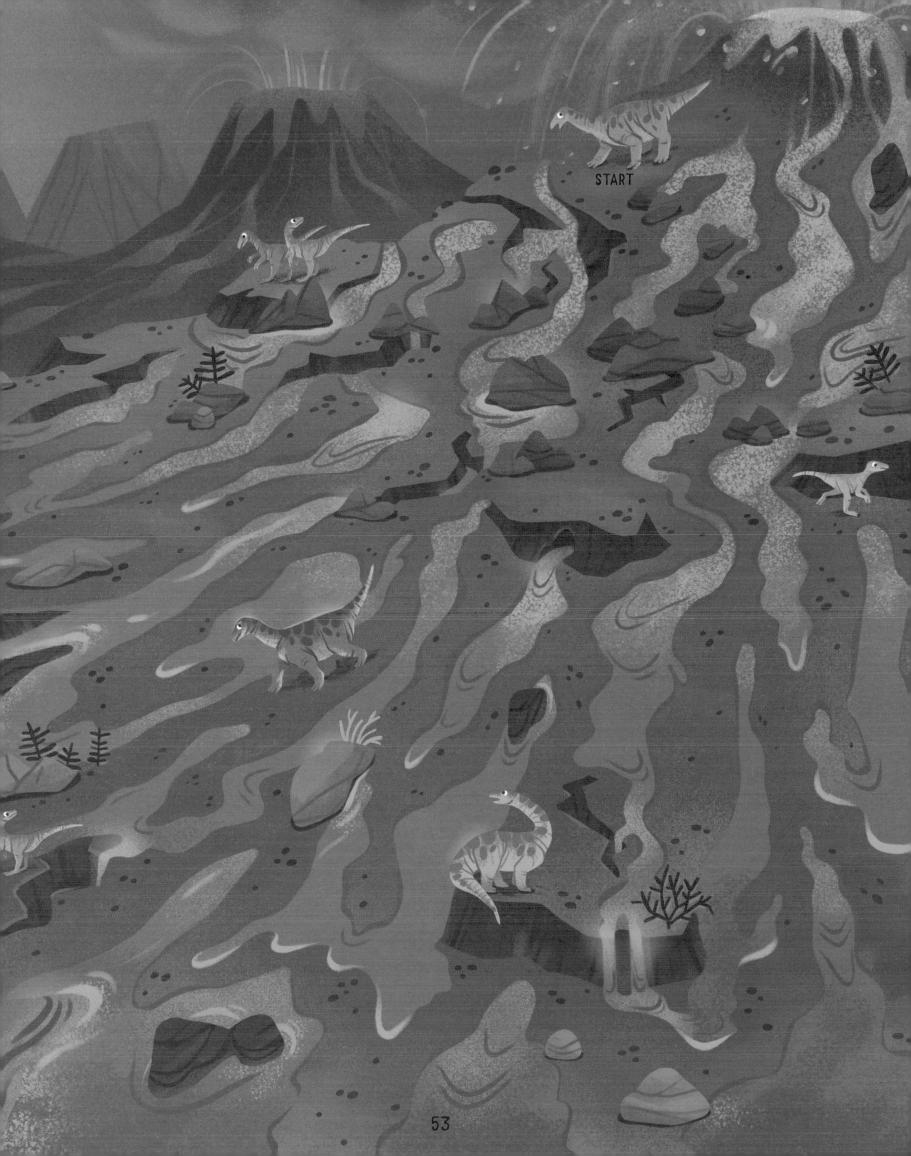

START

Midnight feast

These Jeholopterus are hunting for juicy bugs as a midnight meal. Which way should the pink one fly to catch exactly 12 insects on its way down to the trees, without taking any path twice?

START

FINISH

Long-distance flight

The Ardeadactylus is flying thousands of miles to settle somewhere by the sea where there's lots of fish. Find a way along the paths to a suitable spot, resting at every location marked with a red circle along the way, and without retracing any of the route.

Panthalassic Ocean

Diplodocus

Ceratosaurus

Daanasaurus

Stegosaurus

Mamenchisaurus

Kentrosaurus

Tethys Sea

Brachytrachelopan

Ardeadactylus

Desert directions

Which path should the Protoceratops take through the dry desert to return to its eggs? Avoid bumping into any other dinosaurs who are blocking the way.

START

Fossil flight plan

Can you plan a route along the flight paths for the archaeologists'
plane to land at each dig site so they can examine the fossils that
have been found there? They need to finish at the Tyrannosaurus
excavation and don't want to retrace any of their route.

Baryonyx

Tyrannosaurus

Stenonychosaurus

Triceratops

Sarcosuchus

Argentinosaurus

Antarctopelta

Psittacosaurus

Charonosaurus

Iguanodon

Plane

Microraptor

Futabasaurus

Melanorosaurus

Atlascopcosaurus

Sauropod snacks

Lead the sauropods across the landscape to eat from all seven fertile green areas, before going back to where they began. Don't take them any way twice, or force them to get their feet wet by walking through water.

Sauropods

2. Hot-spring hatchlings

3. Mud muddle

4-5. Seafood supper

6. Desk directions

7. Forest fright

8. Quetzalcoatlus quest

9. Cave cover

10-11. Woodland walk

12. Crowded coast

13. Lake reunion

14-15. Finding fossils

16-17. Swim to the surface

SOLUTIONS

18. Tree climber

19. Fossilized footprints

The footprints belonged to Allosaurus.

20-21. Picky plant-eater

22. Tinodon trails

23. Going underground

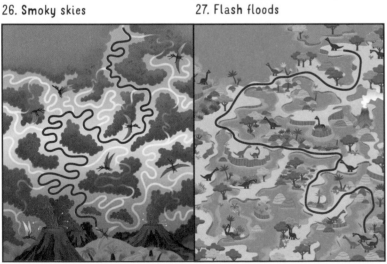

24. Twilight trouble

25. River route

26. Smoky skies

27. Flash floods

28-29. Wintry waters

30-31. Weary wanderers

32. Cave course

33. Missing Maiasaura

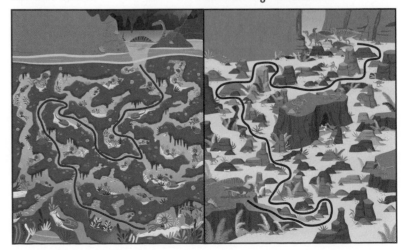

34-35. Dinosaur museum

36-37. Canyon crisis

38. Sauropod search

39. Earthquake escape

40-41. Wade through the water

42. Glade glider

43. Meteorite strike

44-45. Mangrove meal

46-47. Forest feeders

48. Crater confusion

49. Prehistoric Park

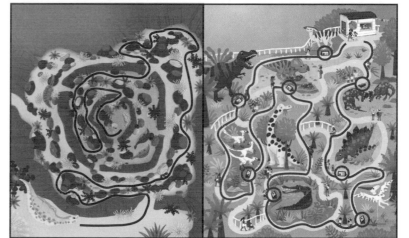

50-51. Lagoon lunch

52-53. Dangerous descent

54. Midnight feast   55. Long-distance flight

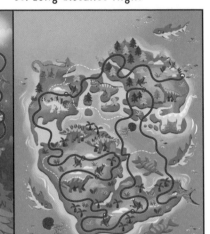

56-57. Desert directions

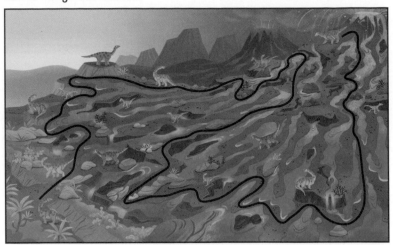

58-59. Fossil flight plan

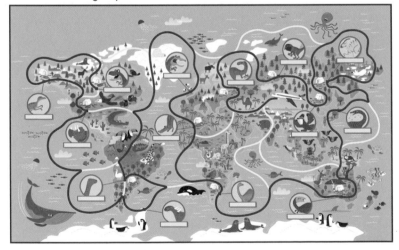

60. Sauropod snacks

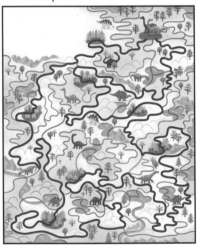

Acknowledgements

Edited by Sam Taplin
Additional design by Candice Whatmore

First published in 2021 by Usborne Publishing Limited, 83-85 Saffron Hill, London EC1N 8RT, United Kingdom. usborne.com
First published in America 2021. This edition published 2023. UE